# How to Draw Dinosaurs

## (A step-by-step guide to draw Abrosaurus, T-Rex, Saltasaurus and many many more)

### By Alex Man

**Book 1**

# Table of Contents:

Styracosaurus ⎯⎯⎯⎯⎯⎯⎯⎯⎯⎯⎯⎯⎯⎯⎯⎯⎯

Therizinosaurus ⎯⎯⎯⎯⎯⎯⎯⎯⎯⎯⎯⎯⎯⎯⎯⎯

Thescelosaurus ⎯⎯⎯⎯⎯⎯⎯⎯⎯⎯⎯⎯⎯⎯⎯⎯

Udanoceratops ⎯⎯⎯⎯⎯⎯⎯⎯⎯⎯⎯⎯⎯⎯⎯⎯

Yingshanosaurus ⎯⎯⎯⎯⎯⎯⎯⎯⎯⎯⎯⎯⎯⎯⎯

Tyrannosaurus rex ⎯⎯⎯⎯⎯⎯⎯⎯⎯⎯⎯⎯⎯⎯

Yuanmousaurus ⎯⎯⎯⎯⎯⎯⎯⎯⎯⎯⎯⎯⎯⎯⎯

Yangchuanosaurus ⎯⎯⎯⎯⎯⎯⎯⎯⎯⎯⎯⎯⎯⎯

Wuerhosaurus ⎯⎯⎯⎯⎯⎯⎯⎯⎯⎯⎯⎯⎯⎯⎯⎯

Talarurus ⎯⎯⎯⎯⎯⎯⎯⎯⎯⎯⎯⎯⎯⎯⎯⎯⎯⎯

Abrosaurus

stygimoloch

Saltasaurus

Parasaurolophus

Isisaurus

Torvosaurus

Tropeognathus

Plesiosaurus

Colors

Textures

Everyone can draw!
Drawing is like music, a universal language.
In this book I will show you,
step by step,
how to draw dinosaurs.

The instructions are given only by drawings,
so there is no need to add text,
that way even young children
can use the book by themselves.

On each page you can find a different dinosaur.
On one page you have the directions on how to draw,
and on the following page the drawing with its environment,
as a part of the whole picture.

I put a lot of effort into this book,
trying to make the drawings easy,
and accessible for all, and most importantly- fun for all!
I hope you will enjoy both learning how to draw the dinosaurs
and the experience.
So... grab a sheet of paper and a pencil,
and let's go back in time into the world of dinosaurs.
Sincerely yours,
Alex

# Styracosaurus

Therizinosaurus

# Thescelosaurus

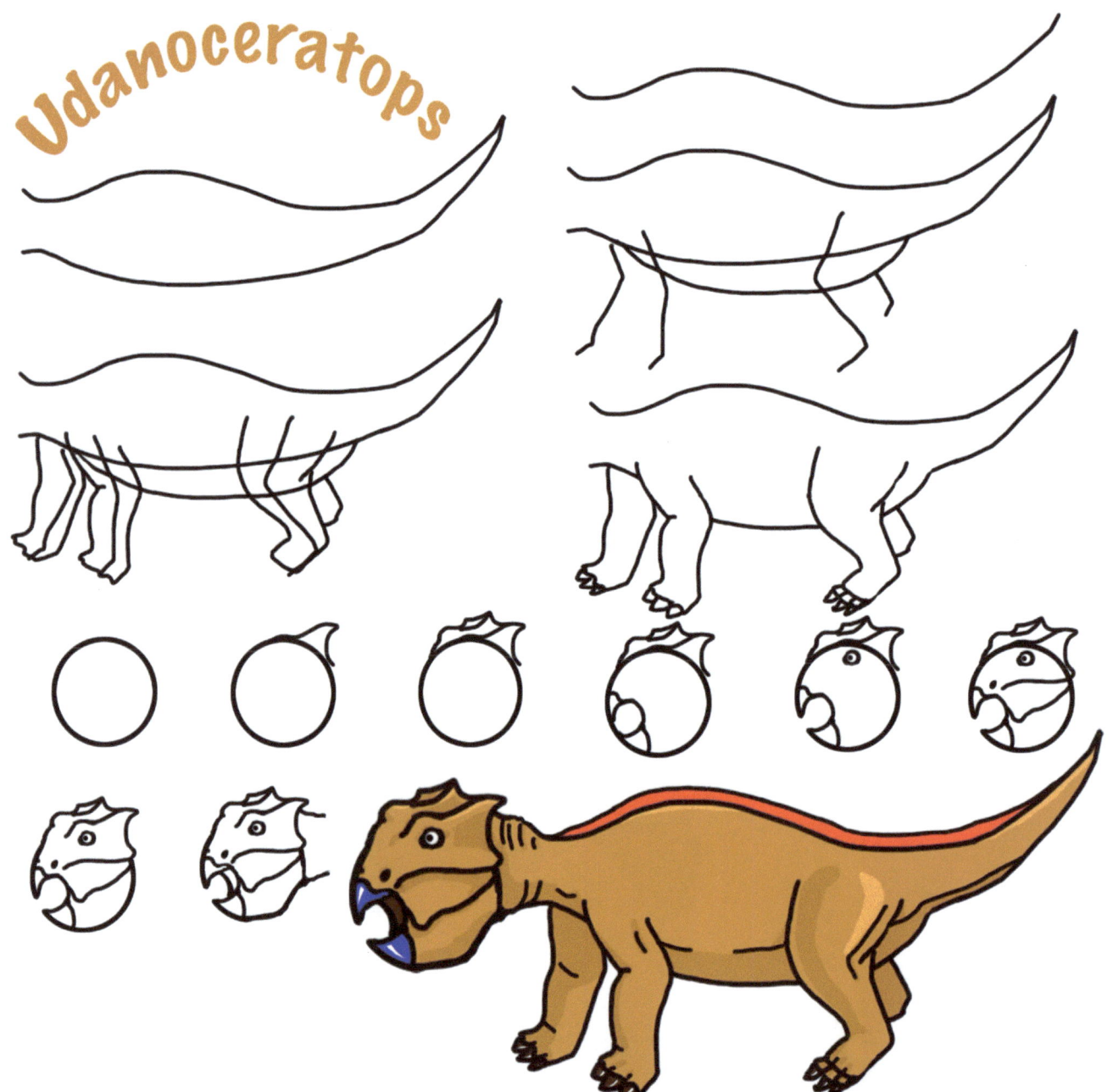

Udanoceratops

Yingshanosaurus

Tyrannosaurus rex

Yuanmousaurus

yangchuanosaurus

Wuerhosaurus

# Talarurus

Abrosaurus

# Stygimoloch

# Saltasaurus

Parasaurolophus

Isisaurus

Torvosaurus

# Tropeognathus

Plesiosaurus

Textures